Dedicated to K.N.

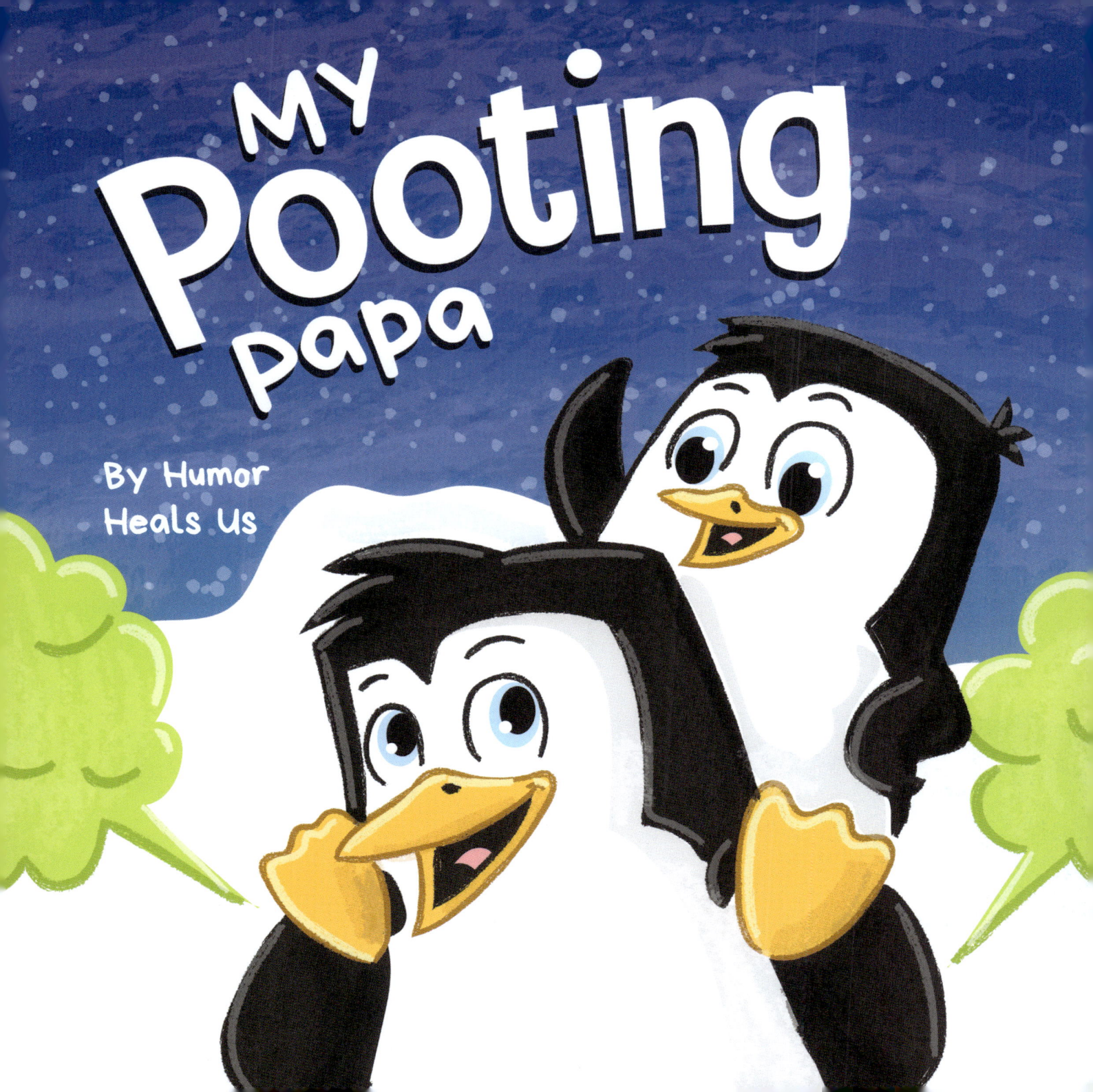

My Papa is my protector.
He keeps me out of trouble.
He teaches me right from wrong,
And pulls me from the rubble.

If there was a prize for farting,
I'm sure my dad would win.
No matter where, no matter when,
It's all the same to him.

If your dad says, "Pull my finger,"
Make sure you never do.
It means he's planning a huge fart
And will put the blame on you.

Our mothers fart and poot too.
Their farts sometimes have no odor.
But nothing compares to a father's farts
Especially after some sodas.

Papa poots are really deadly.
Sometimes they make you cry.
If dad farts in the garden,
I think all the plants would die.

What my mom hates worst of all
Is when dad farts in bed.
She hits him with a pillow.
Then pulls the sheets over his head.

Young boys think farts are funny,
And sometimes girls do too.
Even mothers fart sometimes,
But not like fathers do.

When dad went fishing with his friends
Who were all dads, in fact,
The outboard motor stalled and stopped.
And the friends all made a pact.

When dad reads bedtime stories,
He is the best, bar none.
'Cause dad's farts are the sound effects
That makes it lots of fun.

If a lion roars, dad poots it.
If a wolf howls, he poots that too.
He even does a tooting train,
And a ghost that hollers, "BOO!"

Printed in Great Britain
by Amazon